JOURNEY THROUGH THE EARTH

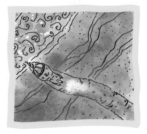

by Joe Adair
illustrated by Victor Kennedy

PEARSON

Scott
Foresman

Editorial Offices: Glenview, Illinois • Parsippany, New Jersey • New York, New York
Sales Offices: Needham, Massachusetts • Duluth, Georgia • Glenview, Illinois
Coppell, Texas • Ontario, California • Mesa, Arizona

Chapter One

A Special Day Starts

"Toby, Toby! Time to rise and shine," Toby's mother called loudly up the stairs. "Toby get out of bed, you have a big day today!" Toby, still groggy with sleep, could not remember anything special that was planned for the day.

Out the window he saw the leaves swirling around the ground over the grass below and felt a burst of energy. Way out in the distance he saw the shape of a mountain through the window. Suddenly, he remembered why it was a special day. Toby finished getting dressed and rushed downstairs with his unfinished homework in hand.

"Good morning, Mom," Toby said with a smile.

"Well, aren't we in a chipper mood this morning." She smiled and poured her son a glass of orange juice.

"Hey, Mom, you were right. Today is going to be a special day for me. I forgot that my science class is going to Mount Randall today!"

"Yes, and I am sure it is going to be very beautiful this time of year." His mother sets the juice before him and smiles again.

"Do you think they will let us go up to the volcano and go inside?"

"I certainly hope they don't. A volcano like Mount Randall is no place for a fifth grader," she replied.

"Oh, man, I want to go and see the lava and monsters inside," Toby said.

Toby sat next to his best friend, Kenny, and asked him if he remembered that they were going to Mount Randall that day. "Oh yeah, I am really excited about this field trip." Kenny lived only four houses down from Toby. They could both see Mount Randall from their bedroom windows when the weather was nice.

Mrs. Cieco gathered her class in the front of the classroom and made sure they were all there. She looked around, thinking all her students were present, and began to give instructions for the day. Just then a giggle came from behind the coats in the back of the classroom, and Maria jumped from behind the coats and ran to join the rest of her class. She ran to Mrs. Cieco's right side unnoticed and pretended she had been there the whole time. As usual, it worked, and Maria giggled again.

Chapter Two

The Field Trip to Mount Randall

"Everyone remember to stay together and listen to what the park ranger teaches us today," Mrs. Cieco said to the circled children. With that, Mrs. Cieco's whole fifth grade class boarded the bus and rode off toward Mount Randall. The mountain seemed to be growing larger as they drew closer.

When the bus stopped, a park ranger climbed up the steps and greeted the class with a friendly, "Good morning. I hope you are all ready for an interesting day at Mount Randall! Let's get started and head to the visitor's center."

Once inside, all the students gathered in a circle around a big globe. The globe could be opened up because it had hinges, and the inside looked like it was painted. Toby asked why the globe could open and what the drawing inside was.

"That's a great question," the ranger said. Toby's classmates were soon all seated on the carpet and began to listen. The ranger continued, "No one knows for sure, but some scientists think the Earth's core may be several thousands of degrees Fahrenheit—maybe even as hot as the surface of the sun!"

Kenny, leaning over to Toby, said, "Wow, the middle of the Earth could be as hot as the sun. Can you imagine what it would be like to go underground that far? It would be way too hot!" Toby just laughed and listened to the ranger. He was waiting to see the globe open and find out what the picture inside was.

As the ranger spoke, he unhooked a small latch on the big globe. "These five layers of the Earth are the crust, upper mantle, mantle, outer core, and the inner core." Kenny leaned in to say something, but Toby gently pushed him aside, waiting to see the globe opened up. Inside, each of the layers was labeled and further distinguished with warm colors. Toby sat up straight, eager to hear all the ranger had to say. *Learning about Earth's layers is exciting— maybe even fun*—Toby thought to himself.

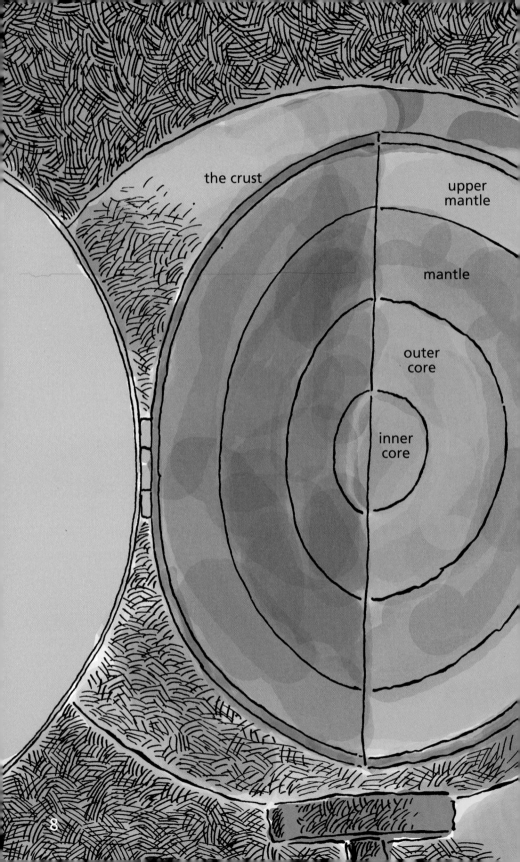

"The crust of our planet is made up of all seven continents and each of the world's oceans. Oceans cover about seventy percent of the Earth's surface. This first layer, the crust, is thinner under the oceans than it is under the continents. The crust accounts for only one percent of the Earth's weight, or total mass. Where the crust meets the next layer, which is the upper mantle, are huge plates of rock under the continents and oceans. The upper mantle is stable for the most part. This portion of the mantle does show some plasticity though."

Maria's hand shot up. "What does plasticity mean?"

The ranger chuckled and understood that he was using too many scientific words. "Plasticity means this mostly solid part of the Earth is able to flow a little bit. Imagine a river of chocolate pudding. This part of the Earth would be like that. It does not flow as well as water, but it does flow." Maria was happy with this answer and liked the thought of a chocolate pudding river.

The ranger continued, "The next layer is made up of the rest of the mantle. Most of the heat underground comes from this part of the Earth. There are huge areas where this heat is shifted and moves around. The scientific name for these areas is convection cells. This heat can cause the huge rock plates, under the continents, to move very slowly. Below the mantle is the outer core. As you may have figured out, the core of the Earth is divided into two parts, like the mantle. This makes it easier to understand because these two parts are not the same and they affect the planet in different ways."

The ranger continued. "Many scientists have researched this part of the Earth, but this is difficult because it is too hot and far too deep a place for humans to visit."

Toby stopped listening for a moment and imagined going through the outer core. He would be able to do what all the grown-ups have never been able to do. Then he snapped out of his daydream and kept listening. He wanted to learn more about this outer core.

"So the outer core is made up of iron and some other metals. Scientists also believe that it is liquid and can flow a little faster than the chocolate pudding river." As the ranger continued, he glanced back to laugh with Maria again but did not see her. "The inner core of the Earth is thought to be made of iron and another metal called nickel. It is very dense; this means that it is solid, unlike the outer core of the Earth. There is a great deal of pressure at this level of the Earth, and the metal's strength helps to keep the inner core solid. The weight of all the other layers above it creates the pressure needed to do this."

Kenny raised his hand and asked, "Do you think people will ever go to the core of the Earth and explore it?"

The ranger laughed a little. "No, I don't believe that would ever be possible. To take a trip through the Earth, and go through the layers we just learned about, can only be a dream. There are no machines made to take the heat that one would encounter along the way. And this is only one of the reasons such a journey would not be possible."

Kenny looked a little disappointed, and Toby had an unhappy look on his face at this news. They both had the same idea in their heads. They wanted to find a way to take the long journey through the Earth.

Mrs. Cieco said, "Let's get our jackets back on and get out to the bus. Next we are going back up the road to get as close to the volcano as we can. The ranger smiled to her and nodded his head.

At the volcano, everyone formed a line behind the ranger. Toby and Kenny decided to fall behind a bit and talk about their idea to go and see what was inside the mysterious volcano.

Chapter Three
The Plunge into Mount Randall

"Hey Toby," Kenny whispered, "do you want to see if we can get a little closer to the top so we can look inside?"

"I don't know. It's pretty cold. Maybe we should just forget about this plan."

"No way," Kenny replied. "This could be our only chance." Toby was not feeling too good about this, but went with Kenny's idea to wait until the class headed back to the bus to make a break for the top of the volcano. They heard the ranger stop talking and Mrs. Cieco loudly call for her fifth grade class to save questions for the bus ride back.

Soon their classmates were down the hill and out of sight. Toby and Kenny, both a bit nervous, decided to hike back up. There was snow on the ground, and their feet were getting cold. They both began to doubt the wisdom of this decision but would not admit it each other.

Peering into the volcano, they saw only a great darkness, a huge black hole. The rocks leading into its crater were broken into small pieces and looked slippery.

"Hey, Kenny," Toby said with a new sense of courage, "let's climb over this ledge and get closer." The two boys crawled up to the ledge so they would not slip. They were as close as they wanted to get as they peered into the volcano's interior. "Well, Kenny, I think we better head back. If we miss the bus, our parents will be very angry."

"Yeah, I think you're right," Kenny replied. They turned at the mouth of the volcano to head home. "Oh, my gosh!" Kenny screamed as he slipped and began to slide down the wrong way. He was headed into the volcano. Toby reached for him and grabbed his hand. Their hearts were beating wildly. Toby held on tight, but Kenny was too heavy to pull up.

Toby reached to grab a nearby rock. "Kenny, I'm slipping too!" The boys separated their hands and began to plunge head first into the great darkness below. With nothing to grab on the smooth walls of the volcano, they just fell deeper and deeper, wondering if they would ever reach bottom.

Chapter Four

Sir Edmond's Earth Exploration Craft

Thud! The boys hit the bottom. "Are you all right?" they both asked at the same time. The boys could only see shadows. Kenny looked at Toby and said, "There has got to be some way out of here." They looked around for a ladder, a rope, anything that would help them get home again. There was nothing. Both boys were stunned with fear.

Toby explored a dark corner hoping to find something. Suddenly, he bumped into something made of metal. He could see that it was a huge machine of some sort. It had one tiny door on the side and four windows near the top. It was shaped like a pear. On top was a huge drill that pointed up toward the top of the volcano. Toby called out, "Kenny, what is this thing?"

Kenny spotted a note tied to the door and tore it off and read it aloud. "Hello there, you must have had a bumpy ride down. My name is Sir Edmond, and you have found my Earth Exploration Craft. I came to this volcano from England. Please do not take this craft; I will be back in two days to drive it home." Kenny looked sad. "Toby, this note was written March 3, 1903."

This was not good news. Toby tried to open the door, but it was rusted shut. Just then, Kenny screamed, "Toby, Toby, look!" There was a huge serpent coming toward them. Both pulled until the door finally opened. The snake pounded the windows, releasing hideous sounds before it stole away into a dark corner.

"Toby, what was that thing?"

Toby looked at Kenny and said, "That giant serpent would have eaten us alive if we hadn't found this machine." The boys decided not to go back out, as the serpent was still hiding in the darkness. Toby pulled a red lever and a bunch of lights went on. The machine still worked! Toby and Kenny began reading the labels on the different levers, switches, and buttons. Kenny figured out how to run the big drill on top, and Toby was able to start the rockets on the bottom of the machine. The machine was not made to fly, though. Sir Edmond designed it to burrow into the ground and make tunnels. Toby excitedly said, "Sir Edmond tunneled his way here from England! Wow, this is so neat! Maybe we can use this craft to get home."

Just then, there was a knock at the door. Feeling tormented, they jumped and feared the serpent had returned. "Help me, I'm really scared!" The boys looked at each other in amazement as they recognized Maria's face. "Let me in! That hideous serpent is still here," she screamed as the boys opened the door for her. "I heard you talking about the volcano and thought it sounded like a good idea, so I followed you to the top and slipped on the rocks," Maria explained.

Toby replied, "Well, you can stay with us. We figured out how to drive this machine, and we plan on being back home in time for dinner."

The boys started the engine. It sputtered at first and then hummed nicely. Kenny started the drill, and Toby turned the rockets on. The machine rose about 10 feet from the ground and then turned upside down. Toby, Kenny, and Maria were belted in place, so they did not fall out. Toby steered the machine closer to the ground, Kenny ran the drill at full speed, and in they plunged!

Kenny was worried because there was no map. "I only know that we are going straight down," he told the others. "Now turn right, Toby!" shouted Kenny. Toby tried, but the lever snapped off.

"Well, now what are we going to do? We broke the turning control, and we can only go straight." Maria glanced over to Kenny and added, "I guess we won't be back for dinner then."

Toby thought for a moment and said, "This means that we have to take this machine straight through the center of the Earth. If we stop, we will be stuck in this tunnel forever."

Kenny's and Maria's shocked faces revealed their memory of the ranger's words. "Toby, don't you remember that the ranger said it's not possible to go through the center of the Earth? It's so hot our craft could melt and boil us alive."

"We have no choice in the matter," replied Toby calmly. It began getting warm in the craft as a small light on the control panel glowed with the message: "Sir Edmond, we are now approaching the last ten feet of the Earth's crust. Would you like to continue into the upper mantle?" Toby read these words and typed in *yes*. The computer responded, "We are now entering the upper mantle of Earth."

"It's getting really hot in here," Maria said, "Do you think the upper mantle will be a little cooler?"

"No," Toby said. "Don't you remember? The upper mantle is just the beginning of the Earth's heat. It is going to get much hotter as we continue going deeper and deeper." The craft kept its course for the other side of the world. The children became worried that the ship would not be able to handle the extreme heat of the Earth's outer core and inner core.

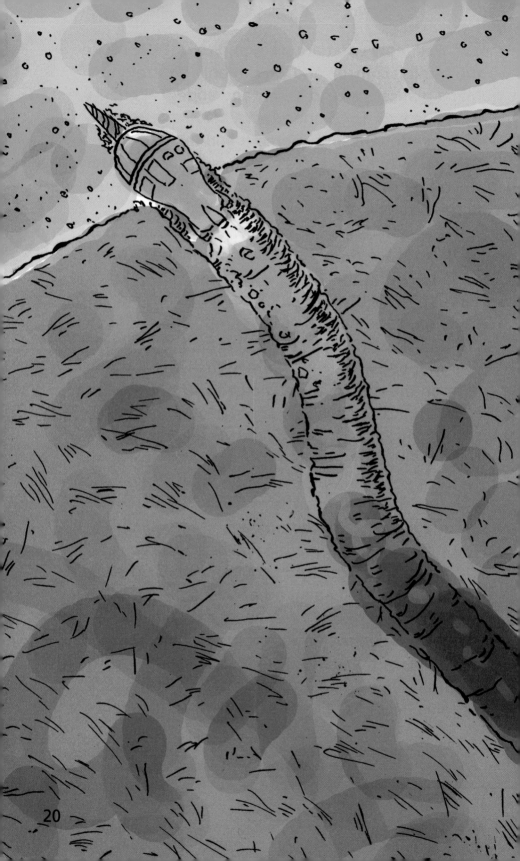

It became quieter inside the craft, so Toby spoke up, "The globe in the visitor's center showed the outer mantle to be thinner than the rest of the mantle. I wonder how long it will take until we reach the rest of the mantle." None of the children really knew. They could only continue riding deeper and deeper toward the center of the Earth.

Maria began to complain about the heat again. Kenny moved closer to see the controls and had a good idea. "Hey, Toby, let's tell the computer that we are really hot and need to cool off."

Toby looked over to him. "I don't know if it will work, but it is certainly worth a try." Toby typed the message with his fingers crossed on one hand as he typed with the other. After about five minutes, the screen flashed: "Why didn't you tell me earlier, Sir Edmond? I would be happy to activate the onboard cooling unit to make the craft cooler." Three small vents along the top of the machine began to blow cool air over the children.

Maria jumped for joy and shouted, "Kenny, I have to hand it to you. The idea to ask the computer was fantastic. You are simply brilliant!"

Toby leaned over to thank the computer and saw another message: "Sir Edmond, we are now approaching the last ten feet of the upper mantle. Would you like to continue at this speed and in this direction?" Toby typed *yes* as Maria and Kenny moved to the front to look at the rich orange glow of the mantle. "Wow, this is so neat." Maria was amazed at the beauty of the Earth's mantle.

Chapter Five

The Children's Journey Through the Earth's Layers

The exploration craft continued burrowing deeper into the mantle. At times, the orange light inside became brighter and then died down again. Areas of greater heat seemed to cause the craft to slow down and then speed up again. The machine was encountering the convection cells that the ranger taught the children about back on the surface.

"I remember what the ranger said about the layers after the mantle," Maria offered. "After the mantle we will reach the outer core and then the inner core. The outer core is like melted iron, and he said the inner core is solid. I sure hope this machine is able drill us through each layer so we can reach the other side of the Earth," Maria said with a smile.

The red light went on again, and Toby read the message. "Sir Edmond, we are now reaching the last ten feet of the mantle. Would you like to continue to the outer core at this speed?" Toby typed *yes* again, for there was no other way home.

The craft entered the outer core, and things became warm again. By now Toby knew how to ask the computer for things. As the world outside the machine became hotter, he asked for a cooler temperature. For the time being things were going as well as could be expected. The noise of the machine was not too bad, and the temperature was cool enough to stop them from sweating.

Toby kept an eye on the rocket controls and the main computer while Kenny ran the drill at top speed. Maria decided to have a closer look around the exploration craft. She found a little door near the floor that no one had noticed yet. She opened it and found a very small and dark room. The boys noticed she was out of sight and called her. She replied, "Hey I just found the bathroom." They all laughed. "I guess Sir Edmond thought of everything," Maria called out from inside. As she closed the door she noticed another one on the other side of the craft. "I wonder if this one is a kitchen. I sure am hungry."

Chapter Six
Learning About Fossils

Expecting to find the kitchen, Maria was startled at the shelves of objects that Sir Edmond must have collected on his travels at various levels of the Earth. "Hey Toby, Kenny, check this out."

Leaving the controls, the boys joined Maria in her discovery of the hidden laboratory. "Wow, look at all these fossils," said Kenny. "My Uncle Pete has a fossil collection. I've learned a lot about them."

Kenny continued, "Fossils are the remains of plants and animals that lived thousands of years ago. Many animal fossils found are now extinct because they're from animals that have ceased to exist. The oldest one found is thought to be 600 million years old! The history museum in Seattle has dinosaur fossils that are about 65 million years old. People like my uncle have found fossils of teeth, bones, leaves, shells, and footprints."

Kenny liked talking about something he knew well. "It takes millions of years for something to become a fossil. For example, if mud or sand encases a seashell, as years go by, minerals sink in, taking over the cells of the original seashell. When it is finally finished, the seashell fossil has become rock hard. Actually, it is a rock at this point."

Maria asked, "How did your uncle find fossils?"

"Well, some people dig them out of the ground," Kenny told her. "They may find one accidentally and dig up the area around it to look for more. Or, a rocky cliff may break away, revealing the fossils trapped inside."

Kenny still had more to say. "Fossils are really neat because they show us what life looked like long ago. A good example is the collection of dinosaur fossils in the natural history museum in Seattle. A couple of scientists took them from the Earth and put them all together." Kenny stopped talking for a moment and examined four of the fossils very closely. "My uncle would love to add these to his collection."

Toby glanced out of the little laboratory and noticed the red light on the control panel blinking again. The computer had another message. "Sir Edmond, you are now reaching the last ten feet of the outer core. Would you like to continue on this course at the present speed?" Toby let the computer know that it was their plan to continue straight through the Earth. The children had to reach the other side if they ever expected to get home. This time the computer said more. "Sir Edmond, are you sure you would like to attempt to drill through the core of the Earth? This is not advised. The risk is great." Toby did not read this second message to the others. He knew that it would only scare them. He commanded the exploration craft to continue through the center of the Earth.

The exploration craft began to slow down. It could not drill through the inner core of the Earth and maintain the same speed. The inner core is very solid and required more energy to run the drill. The situation became scary again. Kenny looked worried. He feared the machine would not make it.

Marie felt his fear, too. "The drill sounds like it is going to break. We are going to be stuck in the middle of the Earth forever! Did I tell you guys I am really hungry, too?"

"Maria don't worry," Toby tried to sound confident. "Everything is going to be all right. This machine has not let us down yet."

The beautiful orange color outside the ship changed to a dull gray. The core of the Earth felt so hot. As the heat of the inner core pushed the machine to its limits, the craft automatically raised a thicker armor to cover the windows completely. The engine took all its power to run the drill and protect the children from the heat outside. The lights inside the craft shut off, and the cooling system switched from three vents to one. The exploration machine made the adjustments to get the power it needed. The little red light went on again, and this time Toby feared some very bad news.

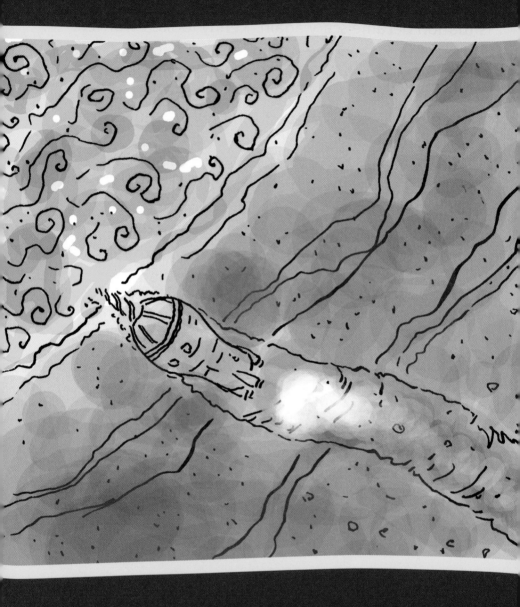

Chapter Seven

Toby, Kenny, and Maria Complete the Journey

"Sir Edmond, you are now reaching the last 10 feet of the Earth's core. Would you like to continue in this direction at the current speed?" Toby breathed a huge sigh of relief. "Hey, we made it through the core!" Kenny, Maria, and Toby all jumped up and hugged each other. The worst was over. The machine had left the Earth's core. The lights went back on, and all the cooling vents began to blow again. Sir Edmond would have been very proud to know that his Earth exploration machine could make it through each of the Earth's layers, including the core.

The journey through the Earth was not over, though. The armor over the windows lowered to reveal the brilliant orange color that Maria so enjoyed. Kenny and Toby went back to their controls. The craft was once more on course.

Kenny went back to the laboratory to see the fossils of dinosaur teeth, bones, and leaves from what must have been gigantic trees. At the controls, Toby was notified that they had just passed through the outer core and were headed back through the mantle. Then he began to consider just what would happen when they did reach the other side of Earth. "Hey, Kenny, do you have any idea what is on the opposite side of the world from Seattle?"

"I have no idea." Kenny looked startled. "I suppose that is the next problem." Just then, the computer announced arrival at the upper mantle.

The craft burrowed through the upper mantle and then the rocky crust of Earth. The children could hardly wait to fill their lungs with fresh air again. They sat silently watching the computer. "Sir Edmond, you are now approaching the last ten feet of Earth's crust. Would you like to continue in this direction at the current speed?"

"Hey, this is the thinnest layer," Toby laughed, "so we should be back on the surface in no time." Boom! Moving at full speed, the craft cracked through the Earth's crust, ripping the ground and hovering ten feet over the ground.

"Hurray! Hurray! Hurray! We made it through Earth!" Kenny shut the drill off, and Toby used the rocket controls to bring the machine safely to the surface. Maria was the first to turn the wheel and climb free, with the boys right behind her.

"Where on Earth do you think we are?" Maria asked. All they could hear from the barren landscape were birds and ocean waves. They began walking, hoping for some sign of human activity.

"Hey, there!" Behind them stood a man looking very shocked. "How did you children get here?"

Kenny asked, "Where are we?"

"This is Marion Island—just north of Antarctica," the man said, "and this is a scientific research station. I can't imagine what brought you children here."

The children laughed when Toby said, "I don't think you would believe it if I told you."

Then the man led them into the research station. "I guess you want to call your parents," he said.

"Uh-oh," gulped Maria. "We'll be grounded for life!"

Getting Inside Earth

We know little about Earth's interior. The biggest problem is how to get there. In all our attempts to drill into Earth, we've dug only 6.2 miles (10 kilometers). Earth's crust is at least 125 miles (200 kilometers) thick. Beyond that are the gooey mantle, liquid outer core, and then the solid inner core.

In 2003 David Stevenson, a geophysicist who studies Earth's physical processes, had an idea. Because Earth's inner layers are made of mostly iron, he decided to use iron to get through them.

Stevenson's plan explodes a huge hole—900 feet (300 meters) deep and 30 feet (10 meters) wide into Earth's crust. Then, hot iron is poured down the hole, creating a crack through the crust. The force of flowing iron causes the crack to run all the way to Earth's core. Then, an electronic probe can be sent along the crack to the center of Earth.

Finally, the last thing to do is create a probe strong enough to survive the trip.